FINISHING LINE PRESS

www.finishinglinepress.com

SAINTS AND OTHER STRANGERS

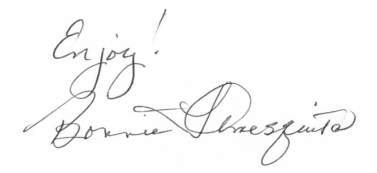

poems by

Bonnie Amesquita

Finishing Line Press
Georgetown, Kentucky

SAINTS AND OTHER STRANGERS

To Ricardo, with love.

ACKNOWLEDGMENTS

I am grateful to the following journals, blogs, and other venues that have
published my work over the years. Some of the poems listed below have
been slightly revised from earlier versions.

Fictional Café: "Girl's Crazy;" "Ironing His Shirts;" "Old;" "Nova;"
"Questions of Faith;" "Touch Hurts" (formerly "How Do You Comfort;")
"The House at College and John;" "At Acme Cotton Mill;" "This is a Prayer
That Prays Itself"
Greensilk Journal: "I Love Art;" "What's Love?"
Heatherhope Farm: "Touch Hurts" (formerly "How Do You Comfort"
Poets against the War: "Questions of Faith"
The New York Times: "I Dreamed a Snake"
Third Wednesday: "Valentine's Day"
WNIJ, National Public Radio: "Memory of My Mother at Christmas"

Publisher: Leah Maines
Editor: Christen Kincaid
Cover Art: Saint Macartan's Cathedral, Monaghan, County Monaghan,
          Ireland by Andreas F. Borchert
Author Photo: Clifford M. Cleland Jr.
Cover Design: Elizabeth Maines McCleavy

Printed in the USA on acid-free paper.
Order online: www.finishinglinepress.com
          also available on amazon.com

Author inquiries and mail orders:
Finishing Line Press
P. O. Box 1626
Georgetown, Kentucky 40324
U. S. A.

Table of Contents

Saints and Other Strangers

It's 3 AM
and here I sit
in the chill of night
haunted by worries
trying to pray.
Hail Mary, full of grace…
Breathe in.
Holy Mary, Mother of God…
Breathe out.

With each bead
I breathe
and pray for lovers and friends.
I breathe
and call upon saints
and other strangers.
I pray the headlines
pray for healing
pray for all who are
hungry
the lost and alone.

My fingers touch each bead
all ten of them a decade
and each decade ends
with Glory.
Then mystery follows
and yet another string of prayers
begins again.

I Remember

When I got the call
I could barely hear
his voice.

A bad connection.
He's under arrest.
Oh dear God.

I wandered into the hallway
then scrambled to find money
for bond

a lawyer
bill collectors
a defense fund.

Months later, I was called from class
to hear the news.
"He's been convicted."

Dressed in orange
sitting behind thick glass,
he said, "My life is over."

When he was small I wondered
how he would look when he was grown
how deep his voice would be.

He was destined
to be president
or pope someday.

I taught him to ride a bike
tickled his back when
he needed comfort.

He was golden.
He gave me painted stones
and sunflowers.

In the Beginning Was a Word

and the word multiplied
begat new words, muddy
without sense
became fruitful.
A generation of words
found a voice
and carried like a whispered kiss
to God's ears.
Dark became light.
God smiled
and called the words
prayer.

I Dreamed a Snake

Today a small child
afraid to go outside
sat watching cartoons
when a bullet shattered window glass
and found him.

Tonight people prayed
lit candles
carried cardboard signs of protest.
Their tears melted into rain
while crosses burned.

Tonight I dreamed a snake
caged in gold
was loosed upon the world
its jaws
unhinged.

Lamentation

None of us is safe.
We are all surrounded by

treacherous waters.
The earth beneath us

our common ground
is falling away.

Standing in the middle
 of this rushing stream

I have tried to abide
in peace on this rock.

I have thought I could stand
safely

and watch while flood waters
rise to cover banks

on all sides.
Now I know that

the place upon which I stand
is eroding

and I am compelled to fall
into chaos

swift currents that
threaten to carry us all

away.

A Memory of My Mother at Christmas

Her long slender fingers
run lightly through my hair
and the scent of her perfume
mingles with the smell of incense burning
at midnight mass.

She points to the English words in her prayer book
while the priest intones them in Latin.
See? she whispers—*This word means that*
as though I am old enough to understand
what sacred words really mean.

Struggling against bad weather
she walks us home in the cold that Christmas night
four children and a small fierce woman.
Her high heels wobble on icy sidewalks.
We stop to look at an outdoor creche.

I look at the blessed mother Mary
then up at my mother
and think my mother seems far prettier.

The cold is sharp and snow falls
but there in the glow of street lights
my mother's hair sparkles.

Girl's Crazy

Girl fancies herself some kinda special
like God called her up
and said He'd give her a job
if she wanted it.

She said she felt it in her gut.
Some people'd say that ain't God callin'
that's gas.
Happens to the best of us every now and then.

She sits around prayin'
then writes 'bout how
locusts grind noisy
how they chew summer heat to shreds.

Well, she's right about that.
Locusts do like to chew.
God made'em that way.
Ain't no big thing, though
and she ain't nothin' special.

She writes stuff like
Deep calls to deep
mumbles 'bout memories and dreams.
Hell, she can't tell the difference
between one and th'other.

She'll sit there and wait on God
while the sun boils down.
'Course He don't show, but
she'll wait like a spinster
for her prince
and listen to
locusts chew.

Don't she realize
that's the closest she'll ever come
to hearin' God talk?
That's the best any of us can expect.
She don't think like that, though.
She just sits there and waits.
Eventually, she thinks
deep will call to deep
and God will call her name.

Somewhere between her all-fired piety
and her pity-poor-me
she thinks she's gonna hear
somethin'.

But God ain't talkin'.
He shut up a long time ago.
Any fool can tell her that.

The House on College and John

Supper time in the old rooming house
on College and John.
Somebody's frying garlic and onions
sour dough is baking
and the smell of spice and steamy pinto beans
makes our mouths water
each of us
drifting toward the kitchen
ready to cop a meal.

We're an odd collection of types
a gay Rastafarian
a boozy musician with his jazzy horn
an edgy artist
a Marxist elitist
a quasi-hippie girl
and middle class me
who the Marxist calls
a *bourgeois revisionist*.
I'll be the first to go in the revolution
he says.

The rest of the house is drafty and cold
but the kitchen is warm.
Somebody turns on the radio.
We hear Garrison Keillor's sonorous voice
telling stories   singing songs.
There's talk.

The Marxist in a breathy voice
sneers mildly at me
kisses up to the hippie girl
the Rastafarian rambles on
about Derrida   the Ren-nay-sance
the artist rolls his eyes
while the jazz musician drinks his MGD
smiles sheepishly
and laughs quite amiably at us all.

If I'm Honest

I want a God I've fallen for
like a school girl with a crush.

I want to meet him
in lovers and enemies

or through the ground beneath or over me
in shadows

and shifting skies
or through the cosmos

in which all of us live
by happy accident of birth

I want to return
his affection

reach out from a place of grace
and hold God in my arms.

Mary T

Wild child
hair of fire
face freckled
damp with sweat

my braver self
the one who dared
to pilfer penny candy
and raid the crazy lady's
jungle garden.

She took me to
the train tracks
that August afternoon
and dared me to run with her
between the slow-moving cars.

I wanted to
almost did
I loved her that much
but the train began
to pick up speed

and I was afraid.

I watched her climb the coupler
then she was gone.

Valentine's Day

I butter your toast.
You pour the juice.
You fetch our vitamins.
I rinse the dishes.
The morning turns your grey
hair to silver.
On this, our seventeeth
Valentine's Day
we exchange
small soft kisses.
You sort the bills.
I check the bank balance.
You fold the laundry.
I put it away
like any other Sunday.

What's Love?

It means I will watch
from the window
when you're shoveling snow
just to be sure you're safe.

It means I've learned to
touch you gently
to stop the noise
when you snore.

We've grown familiar
and don't kiss much now
but we finish each other's
sentences, think each other's thoughts.

I've learned
to love your puns
and how your mind spins
words and dreams.

Do you remember
that late summer day
so long ago
when you held out your arms
and gave me the sun and moon?

Their light still shines as always
and you're still as constant
as they.
That's love, my dear.
That's love.

Late Winter

We leave our warm beds
put on our coats and muddy boots
face the damp cold.

The grass is matted and grey
after its long winter sleep.
We hunt the scent of rain-soaked earth

rake dead leaves away
from buried bulbs whose leaves and stems
push through frozen ground.

We have faith in a sun we can't yet see
and wait for snow drops
fair maids of February to bloom.

Ironing His Shirts

Summer showers turn air
to butter.
Sweat greases my skin.
Radio's buzzin' juke joint tunes
as steam hisses up from hot cloth—
scorch and dry
I palm and press
each fold and wrinkle
mmm, but baby,
beneath your collar lingers
the scent of warm smooth skin—

Rain falls
steam rises
and I'm dreaming
we're strollin' down streets slick with rain
you and me, and some other
cool cats
in ice cream suits
Panama hats.
We shoop shoop
to blues blown breezy, cool.
Oooo dance with me, darlin'
hold me close
fold me in
want to smell your hair
your skin
feel your eyes shine
blue-black-brown
backlit by heat lightning
and orange neon—

Thunder rolls.
The iron sizzles.
Sweat cools and trickles
down my back and knees
as I press against scented stains
beneath your sleeves
smell your smell
all spice and sweat.

Rain falls.
Steam rises.
I'm hot 'n meltin'
honey
ironing your shirts.

I Love Art
—*for Susan Ramenofsky and Judy Rogers*

I love art
if only because
nights really are sapphire blue

and shtetls and red flames
fiddlers and doves come alive
in colored cut glass.

The sky melts easily
into lavender and blue water
if you let the light take over

and white gold galaxies do
swirl and shimmer
above sleeping towns

where painted women
at local bars
glow under green gaslight

and lonely nighthawks gather
for coffee in yellow-lit diners
hours before dawn.

I love art
if only because
brown clay when bronzed

can change a paunchy old man
into a mighty
rooted force

and turn a woman sleeping
on a park bench
to silver.

Remembering Rose on Her Birthday

Most days I can't recall what she looked like
without a photo's help

though some mornings when I roll out of bed
there she is

an older version of who she'd been.
Haunted and gray

she stares back at me
from the bathroom mirror.

Mostly though I hear her when I laugh
as my lover and I dance on Saturday nights.

Chuck Berry and Fats are singing
or Glenn Miller's band plays *Little Brown Jug*.

That's when I miss her most
the way she danced when she was well.

My God, but she could dance!
She'd stutter step across the floor

swinging, twirling.

Questions of Faith

Does God live
in the Black Hills,
just behind Abe Lincoln's stonecut ear?
Or does he live in mosques, cathedrals, storefront churches,
in temple stones waiting to be assembled?
Is God's body in the bread
or in the breaking of it?

Is God Mother, Father,
a Child
begotten-not-made,
Creator made human, born
without benefit of human touch?
Could the Son of God and Man,
combined,
thrive without a coupling—
the fertile embrace
of a creator's own creation?
Can love exist in love's own absence?
Isn't absence of love
what killed him?

Is God One? One in Three? Three in One?
A multiplex of faces
reflected in sun, moon, stars?
An aboriginal dream?
Or is he just another Adam
nailed to a tree?

Breathe

These days when your chest   burns
while climbing stairs
walking   treadmills
traveling the neighborhood
on hot days

you long for air that
comes   easy
without thought
like when you were
small

how you'd send dandelion seeds
flying with a casual puff of wind
and chase fireflies after dark
when summer air was silken
cool and damp.

Back then you filled your lungs
with the scent of sweet grass
or your mother's Chanel
inhaled the aroma of fresh-baked bread
the smell of rain-soaked earth.

You ran to catch the ice cream truck
reveled in games that
made you sweat.
You were free and the last thing on your mind
was figuring out how to   breathe.

Touch Hurts

How do you comfort someone who grieves?
Sorry for your loss
Our prayers are with you
Sorry
Sorry
Words fail
and sometimes offend
Sorry for what?
You didn't give her cancer
Cause the car crash
You didn't do anything wrong
You didn't have anything to do with it

No
Words don't help
They push us away
Bury us with our dead
Sequester our tears behind polite smiles
Thank you for coming
Thank you
Thank you

Touch hurts
though hugs and air kisses are obligatory
Just be there
Try not to cry.
Just share the ache
feel the rage and deep
deep void
not only at the funeral
but months and years later
knowing nothing you do
will ever matter less
or more.

Sunrise at Sinsinawa Convent

The autumn sun burns
as two young sisters
lead us with poetry
and prayer.

We explore
the shaded grottos
a stone labyrinth
and the graves of generations
of sisters who came before.

These women don't seem to yearn
for heaven.
They pull weeds
row upon row
pluck food from the earth

to feed those in need.
They will grow old seeking
to fill the gaps between birth
and death

occupying fields
groves of oak
crab apple
evergreen and pine

until it is time
to take their place
beneath the stone markers
that line the cemetery field.

At Acme Cotton Mill

Portuguese women
three times our age
beat quota daily
packed metal aid kits in boxes
we stacked
on wooden palettes.

Those women went to work
in house coats
bedroom slippers.
The veins on their legs bulged—
too many years standing
on concrete floors.

Newbies like us
summer help
pissed them off
slowed them down
cost them
money.

They had kids to feed
rent to pay.
We were smart-ass amateurs
clumsy, slow.
We spent our pay on fast food, movies, rock 'n roll.
No skin off our nose if quota wasn't made.

But for them, we couldn't pack and stack
fast enough.
Slow down! we begged
when they tossed the metal kits our way.
Não compreendo, they shouted
Não compreendo.

Hospice

This afternoon as I sat beside your bed
just you and me hidden
inside those curtain walls
I imagined the way it was for you
back then when you were home
raising your boys.
I imagined evening.
I could almost smell the onions frying
see the yellow kitchen light
you at the stove, smiling
your youngest boy's quick kiss
     When's supper, Ma?
hear the 6 o'clock news
Cronkite signing off
     And that's the way it is.
These are the memories I dreamed for you
as I held your hand
those long tired moments
before you died.

Old

What's happening to me?
Suddenly, I'm trying too hard

reminding cocky grad students that
I too have read William Shakespeare
William Carlos Williams
Wallace fucking Stevens…

Oh dear.
Dropping names is like peeing in public—
There's no dignity in it
and yet

to think I've grown obsolete in other people's eyes.
Everything I've done
lives large only in dreams
no one can see but me.

I'm still traveling the distance
a long, slow crawl
from old to wise.

Nova

Some say vanity fades
when eyes dim
and hands lose their grip
on closed jelly jars.
Not true.   I am still vain.
I know my blood
is star stuff.
My red and wrinkled face
my wild hair
tell me
I am nova
blistered, exploded
made of worlds
living and dead.
Against dark skies
I shine.

This Is Just a Prayer That Prays Itself

Little girl spins circles in the dark.
She runs, reaching up for God's arms
then cries because she cannot hear
her words
or his.
She can only dream them.

This prayer is a dream that surfaces
now and again.
Here's another one—
In a mirror, tired eyes stare back
weary from searching a deserted house
for secret rooms where
beneath floorboards
mildewed books and baby doll clothes are buried.

A mess of feeling
begging for a voice—
That's how prayers and dreams are made.

But this, this isn't a dream.
I ask questions you can't understand
and won't answer.
Words spin circles, tangle and confuse.
Why can't I say what I mean?
I watch your eyes.
Your mind has moved to another room
somewhere safe and silent
beyond my reach.

When Stars Collide

When two neutron stars collide…
uranium, platinum, and gold are born.

That's not a story I understand.
Physics and chemistry

forces that pull and tug and describe
the hem and fabric of the universe

mystify me.
But I can tell you

I wear my mother's engagement ring
and stare at it

during long sermons
or when I'm beyond knowing why

I feel so sad.
Its diamond

catches the light shining
through colored glass windows.

Its gold encircles my finger.
I consider the stars

and how by brilliant happenstance
they gave birth to this precious metal

used to signal a different kind of union
another kind of birth.

Additional Acknowledgments

I'm also grateful to my friends who have taught me how to craft a poem: Maria Alderson, Ric Amesquita, Katie Andraski, Laura Bird, John Bradley, Rex Burwell, Cliff and Marilyn Cleland, Sue Dorbeck, Ryan Eichberger, Joe and Jean Gastiger, Anthony Kallas, Dan and Maylan Kenney, Rebecca Parfitt, Susan Porterfield, Caroline Quinlan, and others too numerous to mention. Thank you.

Bonnie **Amesquita** was born in Champaign, Illinois, but she and her family moved around the state quite a bit. She's also lived in Connecticut and Ohio. She and her husband, fellow poet Ricardo Mario Amesquita (pen name: Amezquita), have happily settled down in DeKalb, Illinois, home of Northern Illinois University, where Bonnie worked as a First-Year Composition instructor for over twenty-one years.

She began writing poetry in the early Eighties, when she was a senior in college, but she didn't start to take the art seriously until she married in 1999. Many of her poems, along with some short perspectives that she has written for public radio, reflect spiritual themes. In May 2008, she was invited to talk about her spiritual journey on Krista Tippet's program, Speaking of Faith. Here are excerpts of what she said on that program:

"I grew up in a blue-collar, Irish Catholic household, where I was taught that union principles and corporal works of mercy were what kept us safe and our community strong. My parents taught me the value of collective effort. They believed we have an obligation to help others in the community, not because giving makes us good people, but because the health and well-being of each community member determines the health of the community overall.

"My mother made sure we understood that if there's a heaven, all God's children are going to get there, no exceptions. She also raised us to believe that faith without works is dead. She said that if we wanted to hear God's voice we'd have to get quiet and listen with our hearts, but if we wanted to see God's face we'd have to look for it in the eyes of others, especially the eyes of those in need.

"I fell away from the Catholic Church after my mother died in 1971, ... and in the '80s, while pursuing my B.A. and then my M.A. in English, I explored Eastern religious philosophy, practiced transcendental meditation, read all I could on Native American spirituality, and discovered echoes of my spiritual imagination in the pages of Walt Whitman's Leaves of Grass." In later years, I attended Chicago Theological Seminary, earning a Certificate of Theological Studies.

My spiritual experiences and perspectives, especially my experiences as a Catholic, are a part of who I am. They have shaped my way of seeing the world, my way of seeing myself, and my way of responding to those I love. My poetry often reflects that influence.

CPSIA information can be obtained
at www.ICGtesting.com
Printed in the USA
BVHW030211220619
551703BV00001B/8/P

9 781635 349528